César Chávez

by Mary Olmstead

Raintree

Chicago, Illinois

© 2005 Raintree
Published by Raintree, a division of Reed Elsevier, Inc.
Chicago, Illinois
Customer Service: 888-363-4266
Visit our website at www.raintreelibrary.com

All rights reserved. No part of this book may
be reproduced or transmitted in any form or
by any means, electronic or mechanical, including
photocopying, recording, taping, or any information
storage and retrieval system, without permission in
writing from the publisher.

For information, address the publisher
Raintree, 100 N. LaSalle, Suite 1200, Chicago, IL 60602

Photo research by Heather Sabel
Printed and bound in China by South China
    Printing Co. Ltd.

09 08 07 06 05
10 9 8 7 6 5 4 3 2 1

Library of Congress Cataloging-in-Publication Data
Olmstead, Mary.
    Cesar Chavez / Mary Olmstead.
        p. cm. -- (Hispanic-American biographies)
Summary: Presents the life story of the Mexican
American labor leader who helped achieve justice
for migrant farm workers by creating a union to
protect their rights.
Includes bibliographical references and index.
    ISBN 1-4109-0710-4 (Library Binding-hardcover) --
ISBN 1-4109-0916-6 (pbk.)
    1. Chavez, Cesar, 1927---Juvenile literature.
    2. Mexican Americans--Biography--Juvenile literature.
    3. Labor leaders--United States--Biography--Juvenile
literature. 4. United Farm Workers--History--Juvenile
literature. [1. Chavez, Cesar, 1927- 2. Labor leaders.
3. Mexican Americans--Biography. 4. United Farm
Workers--History.] I. Title. II. Series: Olmstead, Mary.
Hispanic-American biographies.
    HD6509.C48O46 2004
    331.88'13'092--dc22

                    2003017252

Acknowledgments
The publisher would like to thank the following for
permission to reproduce photographs:
p. 4 Hulton-Deutsch Collection/Corbis; p. 8 Juan
Carlo/Ventura County Star/AP Wide World Photos; pp.
10, 30, 33, 54 Bettmann/Corbis; pp. 14, 19, 22, 24, 27
Corbis; p. 29 The Granger Collection, New York; p. 38
National Archives/Corbis; p. 45 Preston Gannaway/The
New Mexican/AP Wide World Photos; p. 46 Hulton
Archive/Getty Images; p. 50 Jason Laure/The Image
Works; p. 58 Greg Gibson/AP Wide World Photos

Cover photograph by Hulton Archive/Getty Images

Every effort has been made to contact copyright holders
of any material reproduced in this book. Any omissions
will be rectified in subsequent printings if notice is given
to the publisher.

Some words are shown in bold,
like this. You can find out
what they mean by looking in
the glossary.

Contents

This picture of César Chávez was taken in 1974.

Introduction

César Chávez was a labor leader who rose to fame in the 1960s. He fought to better the working conditions of **migrant** workers. These are people who move from place to place to work harvesting crops. César had been a migrant worker himself. He knew from experience how growers take advantage of farm workers.

César organized an agricultural labor **union** and got a contract for farm workers that raised **wages** and improved working conditions. A labor union is a group of workers that works toward a common goal, such as getting higher wages.

The effects of César Chávez's work soon reached beyond the fields of California. He raised the awareness of Americans everywhere about the unjust way farm workers are sometimes treated by their employers. As César said in a speech in 1990, "Once social change begins, it cannot be reversed."

César Chávez was more than a labor leader. He was a **reformer** and a spiritual leader, too. He changed things for the better for many people. He truly believed in and fought, without violence, for liberty and justice for all. Today, César Chávez is remembered as one of the great American heroes of the twentieth century.

Robert F. Kennedy (1925–1968)

Robert F. Kennedy, like César Chávez, worked for a better society during the 1960s. He served his country as United States Attorney General and as adviser to his brother, John F. Kennedy, the 35th president of the United States (1961–1963).

Robert protected Dr. Martin Luther King Jr. and his supporters in 1961 as they marched for **civil rights** in Montgomery, Alabama. Later, Robert helped to pass a civil rights law.

In November 1964, one year after his brother John was assassinated in Dallas, Texas, Robert was elected United States senator from New York. While he was senator, Robert supported the efforts of farm workers to form a **union.**

In 1968 Robert announced he was running for president. He was killed in Los Angeles, California, on June 5, 1968, during his campaign for president.

Great Leaders of the 20th Century

César Chávez was one of a handful of great twentieth century American leaders whose actions influenced others, especially during the 1960s. Here are two other leaders who worked toward a better society during this time:

Dr. Martin Luther King Jr. was an African-American pastor who led the civil rights movement in the United States from the mid-1950s until his death in 1968. He worked to end **segregation** of African Americans in the South by using **nonviolence.** He led a march on Washington, D.C. in 1963 to call attention to civil rights for all.

John F. Kennedy was elected the 35th president of the United States and served from 1961 until his death in 1963. He wanted Americans to try and help others. He gave a famous speech in which he said, "Ask not what your country can do for you—ask what you can do for your country."

Sadly, both of these leaders were assassinated by people who disagreed with their politics. John F. Kennedy died in 1963. Dr. Martin Luther King Jr. died in 1968.

This is César Chávez's boyhood home. The photograph was
taken during a ceremony on September 16, 1998, to honor
Chávez's life.

Chapter 1:
The Early Years

César Estrada Chávez was born March 31, 1927, near Yuma, Arizona, to Librado and Juana Chávez. César was the second of five children. He had two brothers, Richard and Lenny, and two sisters, Rita and Vicky. Both of César's parents had parents or grandparents who had lived in the deserts of northern Mexico before coming to Arizona.

César's parents married in 1924 and bought land a mile from César's grandparents. His grandparents lived in Arizona's North Gila Valley close to the borders of California and Mexico. César's father Librado was hardworking. He owned a farm and three businesses—a general store, a garage, and a pool hall.

At Work and At Play

The family worked hard, but César's first ten years of life were mostly happy. On the farm, Librado taught his sons what to do.

César Chávez helped others throughout his life.

César enjoyed helping out. Even as a young boy, César was an organizer. He assigned chores to his brothers and sisters. "You feed those two horses and I'll feed this cow," he would tell them. At the family garage, César and his brother pumped gasoline and waited on customers.

After chores, César and his brother Richard had free time. They wandered all over the ranch. They swam in the irrigation canal, a special kind of ditch that brings water to crops. They built forts. In the evenings, they learned to play pool in the family-run pool hall.

Going to School

At school, the Chávez children suffered from **discrimination.** They had the dark skin of Mexican Indians. Because of this, they were often not treated as well as white children.

At home, the Chávez family spoke Spanish and English, but the children were only allowed to speak English at school. When they spoke Spanish, they were punished. A teacher once hung a sign on César that read, "I am a clown. I speak Spanish." Other teachers made fun of him for making mistakes in English.

Family Stories

As a boy, César loved to listen to the stories of older family members. Mama Tella, as Grandmother Dorothea was called, collected the children around her in the evenings. She told them stories about the lives of holy people called saints. Throughout his life, César drew spiritual strength from his religious faith.

The stories told by César's mother, Juana, also left a lasting impression on him. Juana shared her beliefs about **nonviolence** by telling her children many *cuentos* (Spanish for "stories") and *dichos* (Spanish for "sayings") that had a moral point. The Mexican culture taught men to fight for their honor, but Juana taught her children not to hit people, even when they were being teased. She reminded her children that it takes two to fight. "One can't do it alone," she told them.

Hacienda System

The most exciting stories César heard were those told at family barbecues in his parents' backyard. At nightfall, the children gathered around a fire to listen to the adults tell stories about life in Mexico.

The children heard stories about Grandfather Cesario and his life on a **hacienda** in Mexico. Workers were paid such low **wages** that they soon fell into **debt** to the rich owners. Their lives were not much better than those of slaves.

Owners kept track of the cost of feeding, clothing, and housing the children of **hacienda** workers. Once they were old enough to hold farm tools, children were expected to work off their debts to the owners.

Grandfather Cesario saw that if he stayed, he would never have his own house and land. So in the 1880s, he crossed the border into the United States. If he had been caught, he would have been whipped or forced to join the Mexican Army.

César was moved by the social injustices, or unfair acts, that led to the Mexican Revolution in 1910. People fought because they were tired of working so hard for so little. They simply wanted a chance to own a piece of land.

The Mexican Revolution (1910–1920)

The Mexican Revolution was fought to overthrow dictator Porfirio Díaz, who ruled Mexico for more than 30 years. A dictator is a ruler with total control. Díaz used the army to control people who disagreed with him. Big landowners and businesspeople who supported Díaz grew wealthy. Most Mexicans were poor. They did not support Díaz. Workers tried to form labor **unions** to get higher wages, but Díaz crushed their efforts to organize.

Landowner Francisco Madero supported the workers' cause. On November 20, 1910, he urged people to revolt. Díaz was forced from office in May of 1911. Madero was elected president, but for the next six years, Mexico was not stable. It had a series of leaders, many of whom were killed or forced from office.

In 1917 many changes took place that helped the poor. Schools were built. Labor unions formed to protect workers' rights. *Haciendas* were broken into small farms and given to the poor. Many historians say the Mexican Revolution ended in 1920. However, fighting continued off and on until 1934.

Farm workers harvest peas in February of 1939 near Calipatria, California.

Chapter 2:
The Migrant Years

In 1929 the **stock market** collapsed. The stock market is the buying and selling of shares, or parts of ownership, in companies. The collapse of the stock market led to **economic** problems all over the United States. Banks closed and businesses failed. During the 1930s, many people lost their jobs and their homes. This period is called the **Great Depression.**

The Chávez family also suffered. A series of events caused them to lose everything they owned. At first, César's family did not feel the effects of the Depression. They ate food from their garden. They raised chickens and enjoyed fresh eggs from their farm. They earned a little money from their businesses.

But by 1938, the family was very poor. The family had helped others in need. They gave **credit** at their store, pool hall, and garage to dozens of friends and relatives. Credit lets people pay later. This caused the Chávez family to fall behind on their own bills.

From Bad to Worse

César's parents finally had to sell their family businesses when they got too far in **debt.** To save money, the family moved to live with César's widowed grandmother, Mama Tella, on her ranch.

Things continued to get worse for the Chávez family. Their crops failed because it did not rain. It was the first drought in more than 50 years. A drought is a period of time when there is no rainfall. With no crops to sell, there was no cash. That meant they could not pay their taxes. If the Chávez family did not pay taxes, their land could be taken by the state of Arizona and sold. Librado tried to get a loan to pay the taxes. The bank president wanted the Chávez family's land, so he refused to loan the money.

In Debt

César's parents tried to get out of debt. His father went to Oxnard, California, a coastal town north of Los Angeles where fields of strawberries, lettuce, and melons stretched for miles. He planned to earn money as a **migrant** worker, but there were too many people looking for similar work. Small farmers and large growers took advantage of workers. They offered **wages** so low that workers could not afford to buy enough food for their families.

Nevertheless, César's father felt lucky to have found work. He had his family join him in California. Life was hard there.

The family lived in a shack. They picked wild greens to have something to eat.

Librado and Juana had given family members credit at their store when they could not pay. Now it was their turn to receive help. Relatives who could barely afford to feed themselves sent the Chávez family gas money to drive the short distance from Oxnard back to Los Angeles.

In Los Angeles, César's mother helped to raise money by knitting items and selling them in the street. She made enough money for the family to drive east to the little town of Brawley, California, where the summer cotton crop was ready to harvest. They made so little money, though, that they returned to Arizona.

A Terrible Loss

César's father tried one last time to save the family land. He went to Phoenix, the capital of Arizona, to plead with the governor for help in getting a loan. He was not successful.

In 1937 the state took over their land, forcing the family to leave. The Chávez family had to leave their animals and almost everything they owned. César's mother wept as they packed their old car with clothes and a few belongings.

César never forgot the memory of this terrible event. In later years, he said that this was when he started to fight against the way poor people were treated.

Ten Years of Toil

Driven off their land, the Chávez family joined thousands of other Americans who headed to California to become **migrant** workers. These people were called Okies because so many of them came from Oklahoma. Many others also came from Texas, Arkansas, and other **dust bowl** states.

The dust bowl was the region in the western and midwestern states that suffered from dust storms caused by droughts during the **Great Depression.** Crops died from lack of rain, leaving the soil exposed to the wind. Without rain, the soil dried up and blew away, creating blinding, choking dust storms.

Many people lost their farms after their crops failed. Like the Chávez family, they loaded up their possessions and headed west to California, hoping to find work. When they arrived, they learned there was not enough work. Thousands of people went homeless and hungry.

For the next ten years, the Chávez family moved up and down the state of California, doing **migrant** work. In between harvests, they worked at whatever jobs they could find.

The homes that poor migrant families lived in often had no garbage pick-up or plumbing.

Standing Up for Workers

During these years, César's father joined several labor **unions** to demand better pay and working conditions. In the late 1930s and 1940s, the family joined many **strikes.** They stopped working until management agreed to better working conditions or higher **wages.**

From his father, César learned the importance of workers sticking together, even if just one worker was cheated out of wages by a **labor contractor.** A labor contractor is the person who hires and pays workers. The Chávez family walked off many jobs to show their support for fellow farm workers. César once described his family as "the strikingest family in California."

One of César's early experiences with the struggle to organize farm workers happened in 1948. The family was picking cotton in the San Joaquin Valley of central California when several carloads of people drove by.

The people were waving flags and shouting ¡*Huelga!*—Spanish for **"Strike!"** The Chávez family stopped working and joined the strike. They were always willing to support other workers, whether it was to demand better pay or more decent working conditions. They believed it was the right thing to do.

A Hard Life

In San Jose, the Chávez family moved to a **barrio** called *Sal Si Puedes,* Spanish for "Get Out If You Can." Dozens of people squeezed into tiny shacks that lacked running water or indoor toilets. Instead, they had outhouses in the backyards. The Chávez family found a single room to stay in. Eleven people slept there.

One winter, the family had to live in a tent in Oxnard, California. Rain and fog made it hard to keep dry. Heat came only from a 50-gallon drum outside the tent that they used for a stove. They stored wood inside the tent to keep it dry.

John Steinbeck, A Voice for Migrant Workers

John Steinbeck, born in 1902, was a reporter and novelist. He is best known for his novel *The Grapes of Wrath*. A family loses the farm and becomes migrant workers in California. Labor contractors and farm owners are uncaring to starving workers and their families. Growers and townspeople throw food away rather than give it to the hungry people. They fear the poor might sell it, which would drop crop prices.

By 1939 there were more than 250,000 migrant workers in California. Their children sometimes died because they did not have enough food. Steinbeck's book aroused much sympathy. He received many awards for it, including the Pulitzer Prize. The Pulitzer Prize is given each year to honor outstanding works of writing. In 1962 Steinbeck received the Nobel Prize for Literature. It is awarded each year to honor people whose work benefits all people.

That winter, César's parents left before dawn to pick peas. A bus filled with other laborers would pick them up each morning. **Labor contractors** charged a lot of money for these bus rides. César and his brother Richard helped the family make money by sweeping the floor of the local movie theater.

As they moved from farm to farm, the family stayed in the **migrant** camps that sprung up wherever there were crops to harvest. Living conditions were terrible. The unpaved streets of these camps turned into mud during the winter when it rained.

This photograph of a poor migrant worker and her three children came to symbolize the Great Depression for many people.

Chapter 3:
The Struggle Continues

Greed and **discrimination** affected the Chávez family. In California, farming was very profitable—as long as farmers could take advantage of their **migrant** workers. Many workers were Mexican Americans or members of other racial groups.

Things had been this way for a long time. Hundreds of years earlier, Native Americans were forced to work for others. In the 1800s, Chinese **immigrants** came. When they demanded better treatment, farmers replaced them with immigrants from Japan and India. Each time a group demanded better **wages,** they were replaced by newer immigrants willing to work for less money.

During the 1920s, hundreds of thousands of Mexicans fled to the United States from the problems of the Mexican Revolution. **Labor contractors** put them to work in factories and on farms. When the American economy was weak in 1921 and again in 1929, these workers were sent back to Mexico. American citizens needed the jobs that Mexican immigrants had.

Under Mexican president Porfirio Díaz, groups of rural police intimidated his enemies. This made many Mexicans leave their country during the Mexican Revolution.

During the **Great Depression** of the 1930s, Mexican **immigrants** and American citizens competed for farm work. Many Americans believed they should get jobs before immigrants did, especially in hard times. Often, the rights of Mexican Americans—people of Mexican descent who had been born in the United States—were not respected. Mexican Americans were sometimes gathered along with Mexican immigrants and sent to Mexico. This was not legal, but few people thought that Mexican Americans should have the same rights as white Americans. This kind of racism carried over into the agriculture industry.

Unfair Practices

Before the Great Depression, when the Chávez family had their own land outside of Yuma, Arizona, they did not have to worry about being sent to Mexico. This possibility appeared when they lost their land and joined the homeless people looking for work.

Another problem the family faced was poor treatment by **labor contractors.** Contractors would sometimes hire too many workers. Then they announced the **wage** was lowered. If people did not accept it, others would work for that wage. Contractors also cheated workers by under-weighing the sacks of crops they picked. Sometimes contractors took the workers' tax money instead of sending it to the government. César remembered labor contractors cheating his family out of money like this.

Labor contractors often owned or managed **migrant** camps. They had company stores where they sold food and other items to workers. But prices for rent and food were so high that workers ended up in **debt** or with hardly any money at the end of a job. They were lucky to have gas money to drive to the next job.

Backbreaking Work

Farm workers used a short-handled hoe, called *el cortito,* to thin lettuce and sugar beets. To thin vegetables means to pull up very tiny plants by their roots. That way, the remaining plants do not have to fight for space. It is very hard work. The short-handled hoe forced workers to be stooped over for hours. It caused permanent back problems for thousands of farm workers, including César. When he became a **union** leader as an adult, César led the fight to ban the short-handled hoe.

Other Challenges

For children of **migrant** workers, getting a good education was difficult. As they moved from place to place, the Chávez children attended dozens of schools. Many of the schools were **segregated.** Segregated schools separate one race from another. Schools for non-white children were never as good as those for white students. The Chávez children sometimes attended **integrated** schools, where children of all races went. In those schools, other children sometimes made racist remarks.

Theaters, stores, and restaurants were also segregated. In Brawley, California, César entered his first segregated restaurant. He and his brother Richard had worked hard all day. Tired and hungry, they ignored the White Trade Only sign in a restaurant window. They went inside to order a hamburger. The waitress laughed at them and said they did not serve Mexicans. César left the restaurant in tears. Out of these painful experiences came César's belief that segregation laws were wrong. He had this idea in common with **civil rights** activists in the 1950s and 1960s, such as Dr. Martin Luther King Jr. Civil rights activists fought for African-American equality and for equal treatment for all citizens.

A child sits outside her family's tent in a migrant camp in southern San Joaquin Valley, California, in 1936.

Teen Years

In 1942 César quit school after the eighth grade to help support the family. His father had been injured in an auto accident and could not work. César, Rita, and Richard supported the family by doing farm work, because they did not want their mother to have to work in the fields anymore.

César worked for two years. Then he joined the United States Navy. In 1944 there was **discrimination** in the navy just as there was in society. César noticed that African-American and Filipino men were only given the worst jobs. As a Mexican American, César could not get any better job than cleaning the ship's deck.

César never got used to discrimination. One weekend he decided to challenge the **segregation** laws that separated whites and non-whites in movie theaters. César sat in the section for whites. The manager called the police when César refused to move. César was taken to the police station and held for about an hour. The police had to let him go because he had broken no law. This incident increased César's determination to fight discrimination.

A Family Man

César left the navy in 1946 and returned to California. Within a year, he married his long-time girlfriend, Helen Fabela. Their first home was a one-room shack in a labor camp with no running water or electricity. They used a camping stove for heat. Their first child, Fernando, was born in 1949. Shortly afterward, they moved with César's parents to San Jose, California, to live near his brother Richard. They found full-time work on a farm, but César decided to quit within a year. The work was exhausting and he could save no money. Another baby, Sylvia, was born in 1950.

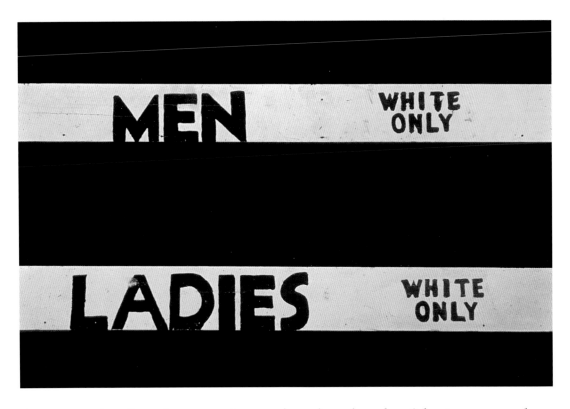

A rest room door from the segregation era shows how the rules of the time separated the races.

César and Richard moved to work for a lumber company in the beautiful redwood forests of northern California. César loved it there, but Helen grew tired of the windy, rainy weather. She was also pregnant again and wanted to move closer to the rest of the family. After eighteen months, the families returned to San Jose. César worked in a lumber mill. He had finally escaped hard farm work, but he could not forget what he and his family had suffered.

Senator Robert F. Kennedy breaks bread with César Chávez on March 10, 1968. César was ending a fast that lasted 23 days.

Chapter 4:
The Shaping of a Leader

In 1951, agribusiness—the business of growing, processing, and shipping food—was the largest industry in the state of California. Even though he no longer worked in the fields, César wanted to challenge the way the industry treated farm workers. He knew how difficult it would be to organize farm workers. Many of them did not have permanent addresses, and they moved from camp to camp. It was hard to let them know about meetings.

Learning from Others

During the time he worked at the lumber mill, César met a Catholic priest named Father Donald McDonnell. He had been sent to the **barrio** of *Sal Si Puedes* to work with farm laborers in the San Joaquin Valley. Father McDonnell hoped to teach them how to organize to fight for social justice.

César and the priest became friends. He and Father McDonnell would talk about the history of farm-labor organizing. César began to read books Father McDonnell recommended. He read books on the history of farm labor. He also read about the life of Mohandas K. Gandhi, India's spiritual leader and independence fighter.

Gandhi's beliefs and values strongly influenced César. The spiritual leader spoke about the need for personal sacrifice. That means to put the interests of other people first. Gandhi's belief in **nonviolence** reminded César of his own mother's teachings. He read how Gandhi used fasting, or not eating, as a nonviolent way to challenge British authorities.

Community Service Organization

In 1952 César met a man named Fred Ross. Ross had come to César's neighborhood to start a local chapter of the Community Service Organization (CSO), a group he had helped to form five years earlier in the **barrios** of Los Angeles.

Ross was not Hispanic, but he wanted to help Hispanic people. He saw the problems they faced, such as **discrimination,** poor housing, low **wages,** and unfair treatment by police.

The CSO taught people how to make changes in their communities by getting them involved in local politics. People were encouraged to vote so they could elect people to help them.

Mohandas K. Gandhi

Mohandas K. Gandhi (1869–1948), considered the father of India, was an important spiritual and political leader during the 1900s. He is still honored today for his use of nonviolence to fight for social change.

Gandhi was born during a time when Great Britain ruled India. British rulers proposed a bill in 1919 that would make it unlawful to organize protests against the government. Gandhi led a successful campaign that stopped passage of the bill.

Gandhi helped the people of India win their independence by leading a movement of nonviolent resistance. In 1930 he led hundreds of people on a 240-mile (386-kilometer) march to the sea to protest the Salt Acts. The Salt Acts made it a crime to possess salt not bought from the government. Once marchers arrived at the sea, they made salt from seawater.

Gandhi's desire to see Indian people treated fairly inspired other people, including César Chávez and Dr. Martin Luther King Jr. They used nonviolence in their struggles for justice for Hispanics and African Americans.

Ross came to *Sal Si Puedes* to find and teach people how to help others with housing and other problems. Ross asked Father McDonnell who would make a good leader. The priest mentioned César's name. Ross contacted him, but César was not interested in talking to the tall, thin white man. Ross came to his house several times before Helen could convince her husband to meet him.

Holding a Meeting

The two men held a meeting at César's house. When Ross arrived, the small house was already crowded with neighbors who had come to listen to what he had to say. At first, they did not trust Ross. He won them over with his effort to speak Spanish and his knowledge of the problems they faced.

Ross knew that the polluted creek running through the **barrio** caused children playing in it to get sores on their feet and legs. He knew about the lack of streetlights, the police who beat up their young men for no reason, and the diseases that came from unclean conditions. Ross blamed the politicians for not doing anything about these problems.

Ross explained how the CSO had improved the lives of Chicanos, a term used for Mexican Americans in southern California. The organization had worked to end **segregation** in schools, school buses, and theaters.

Ross told how the CSO registered people to vote in Los Angeles. If people registered, they could vote and make changes in their communities. By 1949 the CSO had registered 15,000 new voters in Los Angeles. Hispanics began to get elected.

What impressed César the most about Ross was his skill in communicating. He made the difficult seem simple. Ross explained in clear words how people could work together to fight for change. César began to understand how to organize people to work toward a common goal.

Registering Voters

Ross explained that if people registered to vote, they could elect people to help them. César was convinced. The next day, he was knocking on people's doors and asking them to register to vote. César worked hard. For 85 days in a row, he knocked on doors in the evening after working all day at the lumberyard.

A few months later, Ross hired César to work full-time as a CSO organizer. César was put in charge of other volunteers who went from door to door registering people to vote. The CSO registered 6,000 new voters in San Jose before the 1952 general election.

Some white people feared that Hispanic voters might change the local balance of power. They asked questions when the newly-registered voters came to vote, such as whether they were really United States citizens, or if they could read. Their questions scared some people. They were afraid they might be in trouble.

Fighting Back

The CSO sent a telegram of protest to the United States attorney general. They said the people who operated the voting places were trying to scare off Mexican-American voters. César was the only worker at the CSO willing to sign his name to the telegram. The others feared they might lose their jobs. César's bravery in signing his name earned him respect in his community.

The Federal Bureau of Investigation (FBI) was sent to investigate. They talked to César. He explained why they had filed the complaint. The FBI told the people who were scaring the first-time voters to stop bothering them. From this experience, César learned an important lesson: the way to stop unfair treatment is to challenge those who are being unfair.

César became more involved with the CSO. He started holding house meetings like the one Fred Ross had conducted at his house. At first the 25-year-old organizer was very nervous, but he gained confidence as he saw that people were willing to talk to him.

César would hold small meetings at people's houses for three months. Then, there would be a larger meeting to elect local officers. After a new CSO office was running well, organizers like César moved to a new area and started again.

César established a CSO center in San Jose to help people with their problems. He collected food to help the poorest families. He showed **immigrants** how to become United States citizens. Sometimes people needed help with business matters. Some just wanted letters from home **translated.**

Soon César was trusted throughout the community. People knew he would help them. But César also expected something in return. He expected people to help the CSO by volunteering their time or perhaps signing a letter of protest. Later, the people he had helped would be there to support him when he organized workers.

Many Mexicans were brought to work in the United States during World War II.
This man was brought to the United States as part of the Bracero Program.

Chapter 5:
A Union Is Born

César's job with the Community Service Organization (CSO) required him to move his family every few months to California towns he had lived in as a **migrant** worker. César worked hard for the CSO. He often worked fourteen hours a day, seven days a week. The entire family supported César in his work, although it meant they did not see much of him.

The *Bracero* Program

In 1958 César went to organize voters in Oxnard, the town where his family once spent the winter in a tent. He learned the biggest concern local people had was that *braceros,* workers from Mexico, were getting jobs that the local people needed.

During World War II, the United States had too few workers because thousands of people joined the armed services. Congress started the *Bracero* Program to bring in Mexican workers. *Braceros* came to harvest crops, then were sent back to Mexico.

The program was supposed to end after the war, but growers convinced Congress to keep it going, which it did until 1964. Growers preferred hiring Mexicans because they did not have the same rights as United States citizens. *Braceros* were made to work twelve or more hours a day, with no days off. If they complained or tried to organize, they were fired and sent back to Mexico.

Federal law made it illegal for growers to hire *braceros* if there were local workers available, but the law was rarely **enforced**. Growers continued to hire them, leaving local farm workers without jobs. People were angry.

César decided to investigate. He applied for work at a labor camp near Oxnard. He was told that first he had to register at the Farm Placement Service office several miles away. He registered and returned to the camp with his registration slip, but he was told there were no more jobs that day. César returned to the labor camp the following day at dawn with yesterday's slip. He was told he had to have a slip with that day's date, not one for the previous day.

The problem was that jobs were filled by 6:00 AM, but the service office did not open until 8:00 AM. This was how growers avoided the law. They claimed that no local workers had shown up when the jobs were available. So they hired *braceros* who did not need registration slips.

Fighting for Justice

César convinced people to apply every day for work at the Farm Placement Service. He collected their rejected application slips because they were proof that the system was dishonest. Next, César had people hand out leaflets to merchants. Leaflets are papers with information. César's leaflets explained that local farm workers could not shop in local stores because they had no money. They had no money because growers hired *braceros* instead of them.

César organized sit-down **strikes** in the fields. The workers would simply sit down and refuse to work. This drew attention to the illegal hiring of *braceros*. These strikes took a lot of courage because workers could lose their jobs. The strikes were very effective, though. If enough people refused to work, crops could not be harvested in time. That would cost growers money.

Farm workers sent in hundreds of complaints to the Farm Placement Service office. They **picketed.** They complained to people in state government. They finally won after thirteen months. The director of the Farm Placement Service was fired, and local workers were hired out of the CSO office César set up.

This was César's first big victory as a farm organizer. He learned many techniques from this experience that he would later use on a national scale. But first he needed to organize a farm workers' **union.**

National Director

In 1959 César became national director of the CSO. He was transferred to Los Angeles and given a much bigger salary. Now, he and Helen could support their eight children.

For over two years, César worked as the CSO's national director. Yet all the while, he felt he should be helping to organize a **union** for farm workers. The Community Service Organization, however, wanted to keep its focus on working with people in the **barrios.** They thought their efforts were most effective there.

After discussing his feelings with Helen, César quit his job with the CSO in the spring of 1962 to start a union. He believed organizing farm workers was the first step toward helping them escape from being poor. Helen supported César's decision.

When César quit his job, the family had hardly any savings, so they moved back to Helen's hometown of Delano, California. There, her family helped them. At first, they were scared about giving up a regular paycheck. By the time they had missed a few checks, though, César realized they would not go hungry.

The Work Begins

César traveled all over the San Joaquin Valley signing up workers for his new union, which he would call the National Farm Workers Association (NFWA). César drove from town to town in his old station wagon and simply talked to farm workers. Helen stayed behind to work in the fields.

With his youngest son Anthony toddling after him, César would walk up to people and ask them questions about their working conditions. Slowly, César gained the trust of many workers. They realized he wanted to help.

César asked his cousin Manuel to help him organize the union. Manuel said no. He had a good job selling cars that he wanted to keep. He did not want to be poor again like he and César had been as children. But César convinced him they had to help others. César also persuaded Dolores Huerta, a fellow organizer at the CSO, to quit and come work for him for a few dollars a week plus room and board.

Everyone in the family helped César. His children handed out leaflets after school on Fridays and all day on weekends. César piled them into the old station wagon and drove to different towns. When the car stopped, the children jumped out, racing through the **barrios** with leaflets. Sometimes they brought back other children who wanted to help.

The New Union

By 1962 the NFWA had enough members to hold a **convention.** César and his aides showed the flag they had designed. Then members elected officers and adopted a constitution. A constitution lists the rules for organizing and operating a group.

César was elected president and Dolores Huerta was elected one of the vice presidents. They set monthly **union** dues at $3.50. Dues are the money someone pays to be a member. This was a large amount of money for farm workers. But that was the lowest amount needed to keep the organization running. A motto was adopted—*Viva La Causa*. That is Spanish for "Long Live the Cause."

César proposed a plan of action. The NFWA would try to convince the California governor's office to approve a **minimum wage** of $1.50 an hour for farm workers. César also had plans to establish a hiring hall. This would be a place where workers could check in to see if anyone was hiring.

The NFWA started a credit union to help farm workers who had been denied loans by banks. A credit union is a special type of bank. Customers share in the profits that the credit union makes from lending money. This helped the NFWA win more members. By 1964 the NFWA was printing a newspaper called *El Malcriado*, Spanish for "one who protests loudly."

At first the **union** struggled to gain new members. The Chávez family put most of its money into the union. They often had to accept food from others so they could pay union costs.

Dolores Huerta

Dolores Huerta was born in 1930. Her mother Alicia ran a boardinghouse for farm workers in California. She raised her children to be strong and confident, and to fight for their beliefs. She also taught her children to treat the poor with kindness. When boarders could not pay  for their room and board, Alicia accepted whatever they could give her—perhaps some fruit or vegetables.

Dolores met Fred Ross, who was with the Community Service Organization (CSO), in 1956. He invited her to work for the CSO. Soon she was one of their key organizers. Through her work with the CSO, Dolores met César Chávez. Recognizing her natural leadership abilities, he asked her to help start a farm workers' union. They co-founded the National Farm Workers Association (NFWA).

Like César, Dolores was willing to make sacrifices. She worked hard for little money. She worked as a lobbyist and talked to growers. A lobbyist is a person who tries to influence lawmakers. Dolores was a forceful speaker who participated in marches and was arrested many times. In the 1990s she focused on organizing women.

This photograph shows César Chávez during a grape boycott in 1965.

Chapter 6:
Strikes and Boycotts

After the *Bracero* Program ended in 1964, growers could not find enough people to work as fast and hard as Mexican workers. The government agreed to restart the program in 1965, but insisted that Mexican *braceros* be paid a fair **wage**—$1.40 an hour. This was unfair to American farm workers who were earning fifteen cents an hour less than *braceros*.

César wanted to help farm workers get a fair wage. But he did not think the **union** he had started, the National Farm Workers Association (NFWA), was strong enough yet to **strike** for fair wages. Then something happened to change his mind.

The Fight for Fairness

Another union called the Agricultural Workers Organizing Committee (AWOC) went on strike on September 8, 1965, to protest the different wages offered to American farm workers.

AWOC's members were mostly Filipino Americans who picked grapes on farms around Delano. An organizer for AWOC named Larry Itliong wanted other **unions** to join the **strike** to increase everyone's chance for success.

César agreed. He called for a NFWA union meeting to be held in a Delano church on September 16—Mexican Independence Day. César compared the farm workers' fight to the Mexican fight for independence from Spain that had happened 150 years before. Then he asked for a show of hands of union members willing to support the AWOC strike. Hand after hand went up. It was official. They were on strike!

The strike lasted five long years. César had been following the **civil rights** movement in the South. Led by Dr. Martin Luther King Jr., civil rights supporters used nonviolent methods starting in the mid-1950s to protest unfair treatment of African Americans. In 1965 the Civil Rights Act became law. It guaranteed equal treatment for everyone, regardless of race.

César thought that if **nonviolence** could work for African Americans, it could work for others. He said: "It must not be a violent struggle, even if violence is used against us. Violence can only hurt us and our cause." César did not want to shift attention away from the justice of their cause.

The Grape Strike Begins

César first tried to **negotiate** with growers. They ignored him and brought in **strikebreakers** to pick their grapes. Growers were confident the strike would not last because strikers needed to feed their families.

Each morning, César, Larry Itliong, and two of the NFWA's vice presidents—Dolores Huerta and Gilbert Padilla—rose before dawn to tell strikers where to set up **picket** lines. César stressed the importance of nonviolence. In a few weeks, the Great Delano Grape Strike attracted national attention. Reporters interviewed César. He explained that farm workers had a right to fair **wages.** A television special showed the terrible conditions for **migrant** workers. Throughout the fall of 1965, César spoke at universities and churches. He asked people for donations of food, money, and clothing. He invited people to Delano to see what conditions were like for workers. Students and other people began to arrive.

As days turned into weeks, grapes started ripening. Growers were desperate to end the strike. They reacted with violence. One grower threatened to kill strikers. He set fire to their picket signs. Other growers knocked strikers to the ground. They drove trucks and tractors to raise clouds of dust near the strikers, making it hard for them to see and breathe. Some growers sprayed strikers with **pesticides** or threatened them with dogs.

Chávez brought protests in favor of the union around the country. This protest took place in New York in 1969.

Picketers complained to law enforcement, but nothing happened. Local police felt more loyalty to growers than to farm workers because growers had more money and power. It took discipline for the **strikers** not to fight back.

People who had come to support the farm workers flooded the Delano chief of police with phone calls and letters. Experienced **civil rights** volunteers—black and white—helped organize protest marches. The strike had become bigger than anyone ever expected.

More Publicity

In December 1965, the **union** asked the American public to **boycott** grapes grown by the largest Delano grower. The grower not only grew grapes for wine, but also for other products. Union supporters in dozens of cities all over the United States picketed in front of stores. They handed out cards to send to the company. The cards said buyers would not buy any of their products until the company signed a contract with the farm workers' union.

Public support grew. Powerful people began to support the strike. Walter Reuther, head of the United Auto Workers union, came to Delano that December to support the strike and donate money. Dozens of reporters covered Reuther's visit because his union was one of the most powerful in the country.

In March of 1966, the United States government sent members of Congress to Delano to investigate violence against farm workers. During the investigation, committee member Senator Robert F. Kennedy, brother of John F. Kennedy, asked the sheriff why he had arrested strikers instead of growers. After all, it was the growers, not the strikers, who were using physical force.

The sheriff replied that he had wanted to avoid trouble. The truth was that local law enforcement was loyal to the growers, not the farm workers. After the hearings, Kennedy showed support for the farm workers by joining their picket line.

El Teatro Campesino (The Farm Workers Theater)

A young actor named Luis Valdez wanted to support those involved in the Great Delano Grape **Strike.** Valdez had grown up in Delano in a Mexican-American farm worker family. He studied drama in college before moving to San Francisco. Valdez asked César if he could present short plays to the strikers. He thought it would help raise their spirits and bring more attention to the strike. César agreed.

Valdez organized farm workers into a theater group called *El Teatro Campesino* (The Farm Workers Theater). Under Valdez's direction, they put on plays for the **picketing** workers around Delano. Their stage was a flatbed truck that they could move from field to field as they followed their audience of striking farm workers.

The acting group created funny characters to entertain people and educate them about their rights. Farm workers loved the **skits.** Soon, the actors added skits that taught traditional Mexican songs and dances to the children who worked with their parents in the fields.

The theater group continues to perform today. Instead of a flatbed truck, the actors perform in a traditional playhouse built in 1981 in San Juan Bautista, California. Today, Valdez works as a film director. producing well-known Chicano films, such as *La Bamba* and *Zoot Suit.*

More publicity followed as César organized a 250-mile march from Delano to the state capital of Sacramento. The 25-day march was modeled after Gandhi's 200-mile march in 1930 that protested British control of India.

Victory

Local people joined the march to show support. They prayed and sang. They fed the marchers. In each town, the **union** held a rally. As the marchers approached Sacramento, César heard exciting news. Schenley, one of the big grape growing companies, was ready to sign an agreement with the union. César let him know the company must sign a contract only with the National Farm Workers Association.

Other unions, including the Agricultural Workers Organizing Committee, were interested in getting the contract NFWA members had fought so hard for. But AWOC had mostly white leadership, and they had not been very successful in organizing Mexican workers. César felt NFWA would have better success.

Schenley agreed to sign with NFWA immediately. The agreement gave workers an immediate **wage** increase. César returned to the march. On Easter Sunday, he announced to the 10,000 people assembled that the first contract for farm workers in American history had been signed!

Chávez helped other unions fight for better wages and working conditions.
Here he speaks to newspaper workers in the San Francisco area in 1970.

Chapter 7: A Hero of the People

Right after Schenley signed the contract, another large grower named DiGiorgio wanted to **negotiate.** As the talks began, DiGiorgio security guards threatened one organizer and beat a farm worker. César immediately left the talks. The National Farm Workers Association declared a **boycott.** DiGiorgio Corporation fought back. They brought in **strikebreakers** and hired armed guards to keep NFWA members from organizing workers.

A Stronger Union

As the boycott continued, the company won a court order in May 1967 that limited the number of **picketers** near its ranches. César decided that the NFWA would be stronger if it merged with AWOC. The two **unions** joined together on August 30, 1967. The new union was called the United Farm Workers Organizing Committee (UFWOC). In the **strike's** first two years, UFWOC made contracts with Schenley, DiGiorgio, and other large growers.

The Boycott Spreads

There were still problems to solve. Many growers had raised **wages** in response to the grape **strike,** but they allowed children as young as six years old to work as **strikebreakers** in the vineyards. Another problem was that not all workers earned the same wages for harvesting grapes.

Workers were paid by the amount of grapes they could harvest. Some growers grew grapes for making wine. Others grew table grapes to eat. Farm workers who harvested table grapes earned lower wages because they could only cut the best grapes for eating. That slowed them down. Those who harvested wine grapes could harvest all the grapes.

Growers who signed with the **union** were given labels with the symbol of the UFWOC—the black eagle. In 1967 Giumarra, the largest grower of table grapes, started the illegal practice of putting other companies' labels on its boxes to trick people into buying their grapes. Soon other growers were doing the same thing.

In January 1968, the UFWOC responded by expanding the strike to include all California table grapes. The **boycott** was successful. People from all over the country of all races and income levels supported the farm workers.

The Strike Ends

The strike became the target of more violence. It was getting harder for the union to convince its people to remain **nonviolent.** Inspired by the actions of Gandhi, César decided to go on a fast. He vowed to stop eating until UFWOC members renewed their commitment to nonviolence. After 25 days, César ended his fast. Member support for nonviolence had grown.

By 1969 the boycott had spread to Europe, where workers belonging to other unions refused to unload California grapes from ships. The grape growers claimed that the boycott had cost them millions of dollars.

Finally, 23 growers representing over 40 percent of the grapes grown in California agreed to **negotiate** with the union. The strike was over on July 20, 1970, after five long years. César said: "The strikers and the people involved in this struggle sacrificed a lot for the cause. Ninety-five percent of the strikers lost their homes and their cars."

A Tireless Fighter

For the rest of his life, César continued his work for farm workers. Soon after their victory over grape growers, the farm workers' union targeted lettuce growers. César spent twenty days in jail after disobeying a judge's order to lift the boycott.

President Clinton presented Chávez's wife Helen with Medal of Freedom on August 8, 1994. Chávez had died a year earlier.

In 1972 the **union** changed its name to the United Farm Workers of America (UFW). To protest anti-union laws passed in Arizona, César fasted again. So many new voters registered that they elected someone who supported the UFW cause. César led another grape **boycott** in 1973 when growers refused to renew union contracts. Two years later, the first bill of rights for farm workers, the Agricultural Labor Relations Act, became law.

Pesticide Protest

In 1987 César called for another grape boycott because **pesticides** sprayed on grapes posed a possible cancer risk to farm workers. In 1988 César fasted for 36 days to draw attention to pesticide use.

In 1991 César led reporters through California citrus groves to show them that conditions for farm workers had changed very little. Workers had to drink water from irrigation pipes, bathe in irrigation ditches, and sleep under the trees whose fruit they picked. Many earned only a few dollars an hour.

César went to Arizona in 1993 to testify in a lawsuit that a grower had brought against the UFW. In a twist of fate, the grower owned the land César's family lost during the Depression. On the evening of April 22, after a hard day in court, César went to bed at the home of a union supporter. The next morning, it was discovered that César had died in his sleep. He was 66 years old.

Goodbye to a Hero

Days later, more than 25,000 people gathered in Delano to attend César's funeral. Farm workers and people of all nationalities gathered. Telegrams and messages poured in. The memorial program repeated the words César had spoken 30 years earlier: "I am convinced that the truest act of courage, the strongest act of humanity, is to sacrifice ourselves for others in a totally nonviolent struggle for justice."

A Place in History

On August 8, 1994, one year after César's death, President Clinton honored César's memory. He presented the Medal of Freedom to César's widow, Helen, in a White House ceremony. The Medal of Freedom is America's highest civilian honor.

Glossary

barrio   Spanish-speaking part of a city or town

boycott   refuse to buy products until certain demands are met

civil right   personal freedom, such as the freedom to go or live where you want or say what you want

convention   meeting of people to decide on a course of action

credit   loan of goods given with the expectation that they will be paid for

debt   owing money

discrimination   unfair treatment of an entire group of people

dust bowl   any region that suffers from dust storms and a lack of rain over a long period of time

economic   having to do with money, jobs, and businesses

enforce   make sure people obey a law

Great Depression   period of hardship from 1929 to 1939 when many people lost jobs and homes

hacienda   large ranch, especially in Spanish-speaking countries

immigrant   person from one country who moves to another country

integrated   not separated by race

labor contractor   person who hires and manages farm workers

migrant   person who moves often in order to work, especially harvesting crops

minimum wage   lowest wage that can be offered to workers legally

negotiate   come to an agreement by talking

nonviolence   not violent; use of peaceful means to achieve something

pesticide   chemical sprayed on plants to destroy pests

picket   walk or stand in front of a place of business to protest

reformer   person who works for change

segregate   keep different groups, especially people of different races, separate

skit   very short play, often funny and with a point

stock market   place where shares of ownership in companies are bought and sold

strike   stop working until an employer agrees to improve working conditions or pay higher wages

strikebreaker   person hired to replace a worker who goes on strike

translate   change from one language to another

union   organization of workers

wage   money paid at an hourly rate

Timeline

1927: César Chávez is born on a small farm near Yuma, Arizona. It is the place his grandfather had a farm in the 1800s.

1938: The Chávez family loses its farm and becomes migrant workers in California.

1944–46: Serves in the United States Navy during World War II.

1948: Marries Helen Fabela.

1952: Meets Fred Ross and goes to work for the Community Service Organization (CSO).

1958: Successfully challenges the *Bracero* Program.

1962: Organizes the National Farm Workers Association (NFWA).

1965: Organizes California grape pickers to begin what becomes a five-year strike.

1968: Fasts for 25 days to emphasize nonviolence against the grape growers.

1970: Great Delano Grape Strike ends on July 29 when several growers negotiate with the union. Jailed for twenty days for refusing to call off a lettuce boycott.

1972: Fasts a second time to protest anti-union laws passed in Arizona.

1973: Leads another grape boycott when grape growers refuse to renew contracts.

1988: Fasts a third time for 36 days to publicize pesticide use on grapes.

1990: Arrested for protesting pesticide use on grapes.

1993: Dies April 22 at San Luis, Arizona.

1994: Helen accepts Medal of Freedom from President Clinton for César.

Further Information

Further reading

Altman, Linda Jacobs. *The Importance of Cesar Chavez*. San Diego: Lucent Books, 1996.

De Ruiz, Dana C. and Richard Larios. *La Causa: The Migrant Farmworkers' Story*. Austin: Raintree Steck-Vaughn, 1993.

Rodriguez, Consuelo. *Cesar Chavez*. New York: Chelsea House, 1991.

Addresses

César E. Chávez Foundation
500 North Brand Boulevard
Suite 1650
Glendale, CA 91203

César E. Chávez Institute
    for Public Policy
1600 Holloway Avenue
San Francisco State University
San Francisco, CA, 94132

United Farm Workers
P.O. Box 62
Keene, CA 93531

Index